My First

Hamster

Veronica Ross

Thameside Press

Distributed in the United States by
Smart Apple Media
1980 Lookout Drive
North Mankato, MN 56003

Printed in Taiwan

ISBN 1-930643-75-6

Library of Congress Control Number 2002 141322

Designer: Helen James
Picture researcher: Terry Forshaw
Consultants: Frazer Swift and Nikki Spevack

10 9 8 7 6 5 4 3 2 1

All photography Warren Photographic/Jane Burton with the exception of:

9 (T) FLPA/Hans Dieter Brandl, (B) & Front Cover (inset) Animal
Photography/Sally Anne Thompson; 11 Ardea/John Daniels; 13 Bubbles/Dr
Hercules Robinson; 15 RSPCA Photolibrary/Angela Hampton; 17, 20 Animal
Photography/ Sally Anne Thompson; 21 Bubbles/Ian West; 25 RSPCA
Photolibrary/Angela Hampton; 26 & 28 Animal Photography/Sally Anne
Thompson; 29 RSPCA Photolibrary/Angela Hampton.

Contents

Your pet hamster 4

What is a hamster? 6

Hamster habits 8

Newborn hamsters 10

Choosing a hamster 12

A place to live 14

Handling your hamster 16

Feeding your hamster 18

Clean and neat 20

Playtime 22

A clean home 24

Staying healthy 26

Visiting the vet 28

Words to remember 30

Index 31

Notes for parents 32

Your pet hamster

Hamsters are easy to tame and great fun to own, but they do need to be treated gently. You will have to look after your pet carefully and make sure that it is happy, healthy, and well fed.

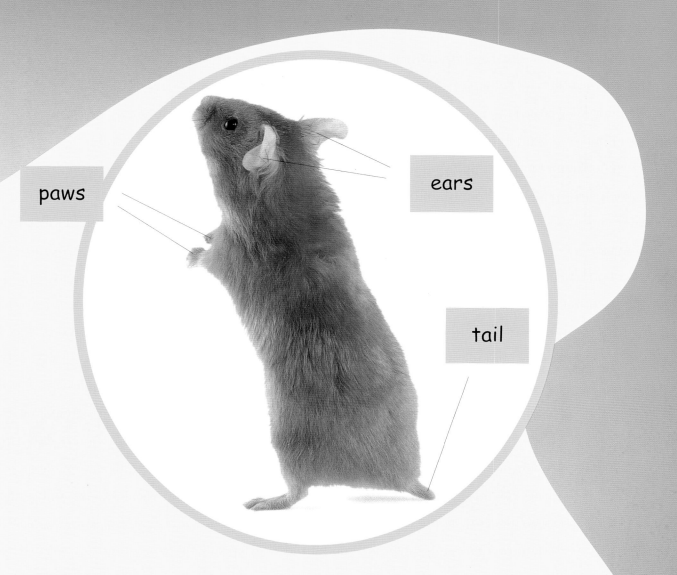

paws

ears

tail

When you go on vacation, you will have to find someone who will look after your hamster while you are away.

What is a hamster?

Hamsters are small and furry with stumpy tails. They belong to a family of animals called "rodents." All rodents have very sharp teeth that keep growing all their lives. Hamsters have good hearing, but they can't see very well.

Small hamsters, like these two, are called dwarf hamsters.

6

This hamster has heard a noise. It is standing on its back legs and listening hard.

Hamsters with long hair need to be brushed every day.

Hamsters are very curious. They like to go exploring.

Hamster habits

Do not wake your hamster when it is asleep.

Hamsters sleep for most of the day and wake up at night. Wild hamsters search for food at night, but your pet will want to play.

Hamsters like to make a cozy nest out of their bedding.

In the wild, hamsters live
in underground burrows
with lots of tunnels.

Hamsters have pouches
in their cheeks which they
stuff with food. They store
the food to eat later.

Newborn hamsters

Hamsters are born with their eyes closed and no fur. By age two weeks, they have soft, furry coats.

This tiny baby hamster is drinking milk from its mother. The milk will help it grow big and strong.

Hamster babies are very small. The mother often carries them in her mouth.

Baby hamsters can walk about, but they sometimes fall over. They like to play with their brothers and sisters.

When they are six weeks old, hamsters are ready to leave their mother.

Choosing a hamster

Look for a hamster that seems lively. It should be busy scurrying around the cage.

A healthy hamster has thick, silky fur, bright eyes, and a clean nose.

Spend some time playing with the hamsters before you choose one you like.

Both males and females make good pets, but do not keep more than one hamster in a cage.

Buy your hamster from a pet store or from a hamster breeder. An animal shelter may have hamsters too.

A place to live

Hamsters can live in
a cage or a tank. The tank
in the picture has lots of rooms. It is
like a burrow where wild hamsters live.

Put paper
bedding or
hay into the
nesting box.

Your pet will love
running through the
tunnels in this tank.

Put a deep layer of sawdust or wood
shavings in the bottom of the cage or
tank for your pet to dig in.

Keep your pet's home indoors.
Don't put it in a draft, in bright
sunlight, or near direct heat.

Handling your hamster

Give your pet time to settle into its new home before you pick it up. Stroke it gently and give it some food.

Hold your hamster close to your body so that it feels safe.

Take care if you hold your finger out to your pet. It might think it's food and bite you!

Sit down or kneel on the floor. Turn to face your pet so that it can see you and lift it up with both hands.

If your pet falls and you think that it is hurt, take it to the vet at once.

Feeding your hamster

In the morning, feed your pet fresh fruit and vegetables. In the evening, give it a bowl of special hamster food from a pet store.

Hamsters like to gnaw hard vegetables.

Give your pet fresh water every day. Put it in a drip-feed bottle.

Hamsters enjoy carrots, apples, pears, grapes, and tomatoes.

Do not give your pet too much food.

Clean and neat

Hamsters are very good at keeping clean. They lick their paws and use them to wash themselves all over.

This hamster is using its claws to comb its fur.

Hold your pet gently and smell its fur. A healthy hamster should smell clean all over.

If you have a long-haired hamster, you can brush it gently with a clean toothbrush.

You can help your pet keep neat by gently untangling knots in its fur with your fingers.

21

Playtime

Give your pet an exercise wheel to play on. Make sure that there are no gaps where it could trap its leg.

At night, a hamster can run for several miles on an exercise wheel.

This hamster is having fun in its toy house.

Hamsters like toys to play with. Put a cardboard tube or half a coconut shell in its cage for it to explore.

If you let your hamster out of its cage, make sure you keep the doors and windows closed.

A clean home

Remove old food and droppings from your pet's home once a day and wash the food bowl. Clean the water bottle once a week.

Once a month, clean the cage or tank with soapy water and special disinfectant.

Put in new bedding once a week, but don't throw out all the old bedding.

Sweep up the wood shavings or sawdust and put in a fresh layer once a week.

When you clean your pet's home, wear gloves or wash your hands well with soap and water afterwards.

Staying healthy

If your hamster has a clean home and the right food to eat, it should stay fit and healthy.

Don't let your hamster play with another hamster as they may fight.

A healthy hamster can live for up to three years.

Your hamster needs lots of exercise to stay healthy. Play with your pet at least once a day.

As your pet gets older, it might lose its fur and put on weight. Take care not to feed it too much.

Visiting the vet

You will be able
to tell if your hamster
isn't feeling well. If it has
runny eyes or nose, or if its fur looks
dull, you may need to take it to the vet.

Take your hamster
to see the vet once a
year for a check-up.

Your pet's teeth should be short and sharp.

If your pet's teeth grow too long, your vet can cut and file them down.

Check your pet every day. If you think it seems unwell, take it to the vet.

Words to remember

animal shelter A home for unwanted pets.

bedding Soft hay or shredded paper from a pet store.

breeder A person who sells animals.

burrow Where wild hamsters live.

file To smooth down.

gnaw To chew.

groom To brush and comb an animal's fur.

pouches Spaces in a hamster's cheeks where it can store food.

rodent The name of a group of animals. Rodents have very sharp front teeth. Rats, mice, and squirrels are also rodents.

scurrying Moving quickly.

tank A glass or plastic container in which hamsters live.

vet An animal doctor.

Index

animal shelters 13, 30

babies 10–11
bedding 8, 14, 30
breeders 13, 30
burrow 9, 30

cages 14–15, 24
cleaning 24–25

food 8, 9, 16, 18–19

grooming 7, 21, 30

handling 16–17
health 12, 26–27

playing 22–23
pouches 9, 30

rodents 6, 30

sleeping 8

tanks 14–15, 24, 30
teeth 6, 29

vets 17, 28–30

washing 20
water 19
wild hamsters 9, 14

Notes for parents

If you decide to buy a hamster for your child, it will be your responsibility to ensure that the animal is healthy, happy, and safe. You will need to make sure that your child handles the hamster correctly and does not harm it. Here are some points you should bear in mind before you buy a hamster:

- Hamsters should be six weeks old before they leave their mother.

- Hamsters sleep for most of the day and are active at night. They can be very noisy at a time when the rest of the household wants to sleep. If this is going to be irritating, rabbits or guinea pigs might be a better choice for your family.

- A hamster cage or tank must be kept indoors. If your pet gets too cold, it may die.

- Do you know someone who will look after your hamster when you go on vacation?

- Hamsters should be kept on their own. If you keep more than one hamster in a cage, they will fight.

- If you have any questions about looking after your hamster, contact your local vet.